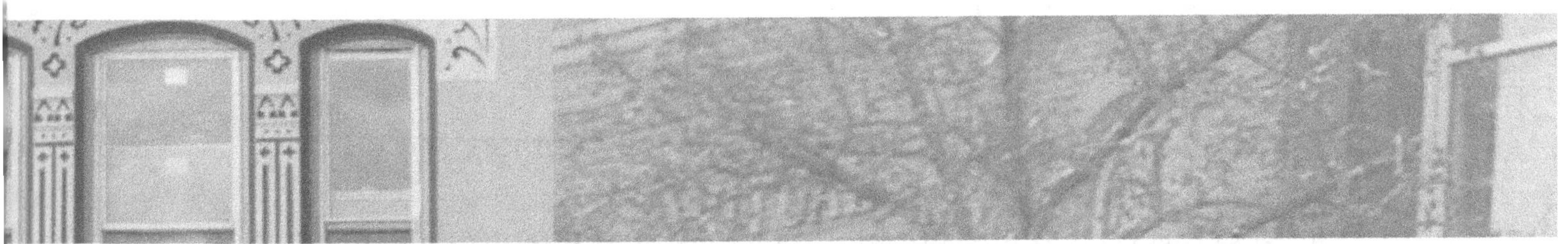

The
Civic Health Diagnostic Workbook

for Cities, Counties, and Other Communities

Sarah Read, J.D. and Dave Overfelt, Ph.D.
The Communications Center, Inc.

www.buildingdialogue.com

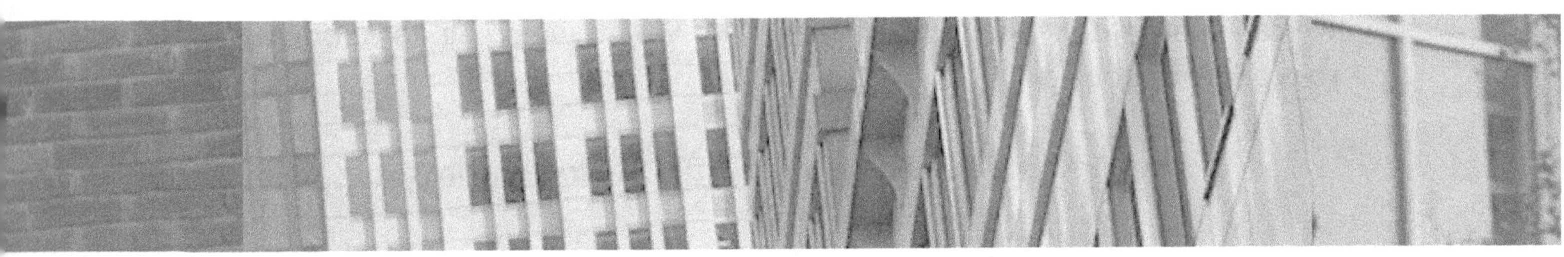

Sarah J. Read & David Overfelt, Authors

Published by AKA-Publishing
Columbia. Missouri
www.AKA-Publishing.com

Trade Paper ISBN 978-1-936688-53-1
eBook ISBN 978-1-936688-54-8

About The Communications Center, Inc.

We are dedicated to helping individuals, organizations and communities with the thinking, communication, and process skills needed to work through difficult and complex issues. We have a deep respect for the public sector and recognize the vital role that government institutions have in supporting and sustaining our community life. We offer training, consulting and facilitation services for both civic engagement and collaborative governance, including services related to this workbook, and we can customize these to your needs. We would welcome an opportunity to work with you.

Find out more at **www.buildingdialogue.com**

Table of Contents

Part 1: Your Civic Health Diagnostic Workbook: An Overview PAGE 1

Part 2: Calculating Your Community's Civic Health Score PAGE 5

Part 3: Using The Civic Health Diagnostic Workbook PAGE 7

Part 4: Asset Score Worksheets PAGE 9

Part 5: Conflict Score Worksheets PAGE 23

Part 6: Sample Calculations and On-line Resources PAGE 36

Part 7: Afterword and Acknowledgments PAGE 37

Part 1 – Your Civic Health Diagnostic Workbook: An Overview

What is civic health and why should we look at it? Civic health can be defined as the ability of a community's citizens to effectively organize their common life. In this context, a community is like a living organism, one that needs sufficient systems, resources, cohesion, and focus in order to grow and thrive.

In healthy communities, a significant portion of the population is interested in the life of the broader community, and participates in some way, whether through volunteering, voting, or otherwise becoming involved in efforts to improve or sustain the community as a whole. Members of a healthy community can identify at least some shared interests and values, and are capable of accepting or working through those differences that do exist. Members of a healthy community generally believe that they can benefit by working together to serve the common good.

Even in healthy communities, however, conflict can threaten the community's "civic health" in much the same way as a virus or other infection can threaten the health of a body. This is because conflict impairs communication, problem solving, and decision-making skills.

In a healthy community, citizens are more likely to be proactively engaged in ways that minimize the growth of conflict. In a community with a strong sense of cohesion and good civic skills, conflict that does occur is less likely to disrupt the community. That conflict will also be easier to resolve in a way that further strengthens (rather than weakens) the community's civic health.

Conversely, where health is not as sound, it can be difficult for community leaders to proactively engage citizens. When a controversy does arise, misinformation can take root quickly, partisan divides can quickly form, and further declines in the community's civic health can easily occur.

Many commentators have pointed to declines in the civic health of our communities. In Hope Unraveled, (2005), Richard Harwood cited a breakdown in community as one of the core problems for our country, and argued that

> "If people once gave their leaders and fellow citizens the benefit of the doubt, now people withhold their support until leaders and fellow citizens prove their worthiness. This attitude has an enormously corrosive effect on society, leading people to wonder at each turn about the veracity of public statements and the sincerity of endeavors by others, and to waver in their own commitment to the public realm" (p 24).

In The Magic of Dialogue, (1999), Daniel Yankelovich observed that

> "Many of the social bonds that once unified us as a people now appear to be eroding. Average Americans, opinion polls show, suspect that our population is growing apart. Americans sense that civility and respect for one another are losing ground. People feel that dignity and sense of self-worth are being assaulted in countless ways, small and large" (p 29).

More recently in 2011, Public Agenda issued a thought-provoking report on public trust in community leaders: Don't Count Us Out: How An Overreliance On Accountability Could Undermine The Public's Confidence In Schools, Business, Government and More.

While a decline in the civic health in our communities can be traced to many sources, one often overlooked source is citizens' lack of knowledge about their government and how government structures are designed to work. In addition to the listening, thinking, articulation, and other skills that are necessary for effective participation in civic life, citizens need a shared understanding of both the structure and role of government in order to be productive community partners. Community leaders can help citizens to both build skills and improve their collective problem-solving capacity by offering a range of opportunities for dialogue and engagement.

Research confirms the benefits of citizen engagement for civic health[1]. Positive outcomes of civic engagement include:

- increases in citizens' participation in civic processes,
- increased capacity for collective action,
- enhanced responsiveness of government, and
- greater social cohesion across groups within a community.

(Gaventa and Barrett, 25). Research also confirms that, if poorly handled, civic engagement processes can harm civic health by further eroding trust between citizens and their government, reinforcing existing divisions within a community, and even inviting political retaliation. (Id.)

How will using this workbook help us diagnose and address civic health? The summaries, scales, and scoring in the workbook were specifically designed to help public officials turn their subjective interpretations of community strengths and weaknesses into a data set that allows for:

- early identification of potential threats to policy development or implementation;

1 Gaventa and Barrett, Oct 2010. *So What Difference Does it Make? Mapping the Outcomes of Citizen Engagement*. Institute of Development Studies.

- productive and effective intervention when conflicts do arise;
- a predictive estimate of how difficult or complex a given engagement process might be, and
- identification of ways to improve, or restore, their community's civic health.

There are very few tools available today that help measure the effectiveness of various engagement processes in different situations, or that allow for the identification, benchmarking, and "sharing" of best practices in promoting civic health[2]. This workbook is designed to help fill that gap. The worksheets will help you evaluate your community's current "civic health", its resiliency to conflict, and its strengths and weaknesses, so that you are better able to plan and implement measures that improve or maintain civic health.

How does this "diagnostic" work? In using this diagnostic, you will analyze both "assets" and "conflicts" within your community in an integrated way. "Assets" include process skills, shared knowledge, adequate resources, and other factors that contribute to a healthy community. You will also evaluate the sources and intensity of "conflicts" within your community as factors that detract from civic health.[3] "Conflict," as defined for this workbook, means a significant difference among two or more groups within the community that causes tension and friction between them, raises emotions in the broader community, and erodes trust among community members. This can be a difference in interests, information, or values, or a difference in the understanding of relationships or how things do or "should" work, or some combination of these factors.

The workbook's focus on "assets" and "conflicts" reflects the fact that a community's ability to work through conflict is a key indicator of its civic health. Although, every community experiences conflict, communities that have strong "assets" such as a shared vision, strong sense of community, and good communal problem solving skills, can move relatively smoothly through even difficult conflicts. Other communities, with fewer assets, will struggle to resolve or move through lesser conflicts, and may even find the conflicts multiplying. Without an integrated analysis of assets and conflicts, a community's "civic health" can easily be misdiagnosed.

The overall scoring process integrates the data from the worksheets into a consistent set of numbers that can be combined and compared for monitoring and evaluation. In designing the formula we used three criteria – the formula needed to (i) make mathematical sense, (ii) make political sense, and (iii) be relatively simple to use. The

2 U.N. World Public Sector Report, 2008. *People Matter: Civic Engagement in Public Governance*.

3 The National Conference on Citizenship has since 2006 published a "Civic Health Index" which focuses on some of the factors that are also included in our asset section. That Index does not, however, incorporate the range of assets, or the conflict factors set forth in this workbook, and does not provide for an integrated analysis of the two.

math itself is largely organized to create a consistency that allows for the merging of asset and conflict scores into one overall "civic health diagnostic score". We experimented with a range of approaches and believe the one presented in this workbook best meets all three criteria. The basic equation is:

$$\textbf{Civic Health Diagnostic Score} = \frac{\textbf{Asset Score} - \textbf{Conflict Score}}{\textbf{10}}$$

Each component of this equation is described further in Part 2. Part 3 summarizes the ways on which you could use this workbook to improve civic health in your community. Worksheets for calculating the Asset Score are provided in Part 4 and worksheets for calculating the Conflict Score are provided in Part 5. Part 6 explains how to download various on-line resources, including worksheet examples for two different hypothetical communities and a list of on-line resources. A list of other resources that influenced our thinking in developing this workbook are set forth in the Afterword, Part 7.

More about the development of this workbook: Overall this workbook reflects more than of 25 years of experience in conflict resolution, which includes work on many large policy issues. The key factors for analysis presented in this workbook, both for assets and for conflict, reflect the five core sources of conflict that are widely recognized in the field of conflict resolution. The workbook also reflects our background in theory and research from several academic fields, and our work with local governments. It was through that work that we realized that there were few tools for helping either city and county staff and officials, or the public, talk about and work through these trust and capacity-related issues in a coherent, consistent, and comparable way. Yet these are the issues that make progress likely or unlikely on the specific policy issues or choices that are identified for discussion. So it seemed that there would be a great benefit in developing a tool that would help those responsible for engaging citizens to systematically assess something as subjective as trust in local government.

We wish you and your community well as you work with this tool.

Part 2: Calculating Your Community's Civic Health Score

The "Civic Health Diagnostic Score", or "CHDS", has two component parts: an Asset Score which provides a measure of base health, and a Conflict Score which reflects both the number and intensity of the conflicts that can threaten a community's civic health. When calculating the CHDS, the Conflict Score is subtracted from the Asset Score and the resulting sum is divided by 10 to place it on the continuum which runs from "Robust" to "Failing". The basic formula is as follows:

$$\textbf{Civic Health Diagnostic Score} = \frac{\textbf{Asset Score} - \textbf{Conflict Score}}{\textbf{10}}$$

Part 4 of this workbook provides step by step instructions for calculating your community's Asset Score. Part 5 will help you calculate your Conflict Score. After going through the worksheets, fill in the values and calculate your overall Civic Health Diagnostic Score here:

AS_____ - CS ___ = _____ /10 = CHDS_____

Then locate your score on the continuum below:

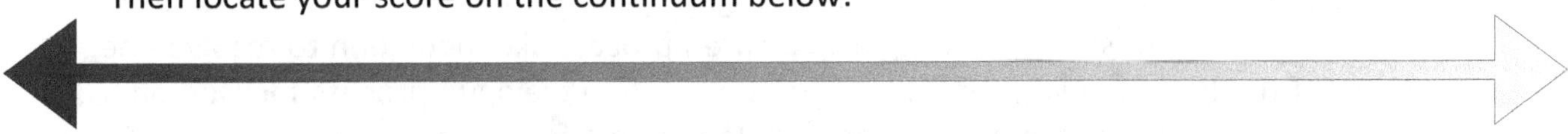

Failing	Impaired	Average	Good	Robust
-10		0		+10

Robust Civic Health is characterized by a strong sense of community, clear vision, strong leadership, easy flow of information and both the demonstrated ability and willingness to work through those conflicts that do arise, particularly difficult conflicts. There are very few, if any, significant ongoing conflicts that disrupt the robust community. This is a community that is easy to collaborate with and ready to be empowered to make many decisions for themselves through civic engagement processes.

Good Civic Health is characterized by a high number of assets and some past success in navigating conflicts. Serious conflicts are few in number, although those that do arise are disruptive and the community and its leaders may avoid addressing more difficult issues until an eruption occurs. Many community leaders and members have the skills needed to engage in dialogue. However, some members of the community may not be engaged or may not have the capacity to engage effectively. This is a community that can partner with its government in many respects. However, ongoing efforts to engage the public in processes that both inform and invite input, efforts to equip additional members to effectively engage, and the use of partnerships between government and citizens in developing and implementing policies, would further strengthen the community.

Average Civic Health is characterized by some assets and some ongoing or recurring conflict. Past efforts at using public engagement have been limited with mixed success. Either serious conflicts tend to recur in certain areas although they are relatively few in number, or there are several ongoing conflicts with low intensity. The community and its leaders do not have a consistent approach to conflict but most are well meaning. Some community leaders and members have the skills needed to engage in dialogue, however, many do not engage and others do not have the capacity to engage effectively. This is a community that would benefit from intentional practice with civic engagement processes through informational sessions and other dialogues that build skills and relationships, before additional conflicts arise.

Impaired Civic Health is characterized by a combination of low assets and either entrenched conflict with growing resentments that erupt from time to time, or highly intense conflicts that periodically occur. Few leaders are trusted across the community. Although some in the community may have the skills and willingness to engage in productive dialogue, most do not and others specifically favor oppositional, partisan, or debate oriented approaches. If your community has low assets, it would be helpful to focus on skill building before you begin engaging your community in an issue-based dialogue process. Consider also using a structured process like mediation to resolve one or more of the long standing conflicts. If you do create a dialogue process focused on a low conflict issue, try to leverage that process to create a few cooperative coalitions. By beginning to build trust among members of your community you can expand upon that trust. Remember though that trust is hard won and easily lost! Dialogues need to be carefully planned and have clearly stated, and achievable goals and objectives, particularly when civic health is impaired.

Failing Civic Health is characterized by high levels of intense conflict and few assets with which to create a collaborative environment, or virtually no assets and a widespread general disengagement from others in the community. Either case reflects a significant and widespread distrust in civic life. There is virtually no sense of shared values or interests among members of the community. Community members and leaders behave in a highly partisan manner, using exaggerated and accusatory language to differentiate their views from those with whom they disagree. Members of the community have limited interest in working productively with their government, although they may have high expectations of the services government should deliver, and anger over perceived shortcomings. If your community is here and you are considering engaging with your community on any given issue, you need to start slow. Dialogues must be carefully planned and structured to mitigate the potential for eruptions of anger or fear. Meetings organized toward the delivery of information and general surveys are good ways to start understanding your community and how to move forward.

Part 3: Using The Civic Health Diagnostic Workbook

Your Civic Health Diagnostic Workbook can be used in several different ways.

First, the workbook is *a diagnostic tool*. The analytic framework used in calculating the Civic Health Diagnostic Score (CHDS) will give you greater insight into the source and intensity of conflicts, and the assets you have for responding. You will be better able to understand the underlying causes of conflict and the interactions between conflicts. This analysis will help you evaluate where, when, and how to best respond to those conflicts. If you are considering a civic engagement process, like visioning, the analysis set forth in the workbook will help you critically assess if the time is right and if your community is ready to move forward.

Second, the CHDS can be *used for monitoring and evaluation*. If the CHDS is calculated regularly, you will be able to determine whether civic health is improving or declining, and identify the causes of the change. You will be able to correlate the effects of various engagement processes with changes in the CHDS, and align evaluation tools used in the processes themselves with data used in calculating the CHDS. Even if the overall score does not change, regular evaluation will allow you to identify subtle shifts in assets, or number and intensity of conflicts, that may provide an early warning of changes to come.

Third, the CHDS provides *a foundation for planning*. You can use data underlying the CHDS to determine what level of engagement is likely to be most effective, identify potential partners, and also to avoid likely conflict triggers. For example, if you have more conflicts than you can count, it is probably not the time to engage in a dialogue process aimed at reaching a consensus solution. Because success with one engagement process, even small, can provide the trust upon which to build more extensive involvement and participation, it would be helpful to plan a series of initial smaller dialogues where progress is likely, before tackling more complex or intense issues. As another example, where civic health is "Good", but not "Robust", you could build strength and resiliency with interventions that promote healthy relationships and clear communication, or that reinforce or build additional skills, and so minimize unproductive conflict. Such interventions include training in neighborhood leadership and strengthening of neighborhood associations, or institution of an ombudsman program in areas where tension is evident. These worksheets will help you with that planning.

Fourth, the CHDS can *help you communicate with both internal and external audiences.* The process of calculating that score can, for example, be used to train those in government on working with (and through) conflict. It can also be used as a tool for building a common language to identify and address issues. It can be used to orient newcomers to an engagement process. Finally, if worked through with multiple groups, calculating the score can serve as a foundation for dialogue about community.

General Notes – Going Forward:

How we can use the workbook:

Who we might work with:

Issues that concern us:

Part 4: Asset Score Worksheets

"Asset", as used here, means a resource that you or others in the community can access to work through issues and problems in a productive way. When productively approached, conflict allows for learning and growth. When conflict is not well resolved, it adversely affects the community's ability to work together. Forms 4-1 through 4-10 will help you evaluate the different sources of community assets. These asset sources are

- information,
- monetary or in-kind resources,
- process skills,
- relationships,
- shared vision,
- sense of community,
- past experience,
- leadership,
- systems, and
- civic participation.

The more assets a community has, the better equipped it is to work through the conflicts that do occur. As you identify your community's assets, also note those instances where you *lack* assets and instances where assets can be strengthened. You can improve your community's resilience and help minimize the potential for conflict by working to increase assets even when conflict is low.

Each worksheet identifies an asset source and then asks you to rate the source on a scale of 1 to 5. The worksheets also provide space for recording notes that will help you track assets over time and plan for effective engagement.

Information		Past Experiences		Vision
Participation	Resources	Sense of Community	Leadership	
Strong Systems		Process Skills		Networks

¤ Assets Build A Strong Foundation ¤

Worksheet 4-1

Asset Source 1: Information

What type of information is regularly made available within the community? How is it accessed? How easily can it be accessed? Is it available in different formats and from different sources? Are easily understood summaries that place detailed information into relevant contexts regularly made available? How accurately do media or other community resources report information? Are politics covered by the media on a winner-loser basis or does coverage reflect the complexity of the issues? What information sources do citizens primarily rely on when conflicts arise? After assessing the amount and quality of data available to the public, its ease of access, and the extent to which this information is seen as useful or trustworthy, rate the strength of this source by circling a number between 1 and 5. Make notes on the thinking that supports your rating in the chart below.

Minimal		Adequate		Resource Rich
1	2	3	4	5

Information Resource	Who Provides and Who Uses	How Reliable

Worksheet 4-2

Asset Source 2: Monetary and In-Kind Resources

What resources do you have to support a collaborative or other problem solving process? Are there funds for rooms, technology, outreach, training, translators, transportation, consultants or staff? Can some funding needs be met through in-kind donation of resources? Is money for public engagement regularly budgeted or does it need to be reallocated from other sources? After assessing the nature and types of monetary and in-kind resources that might be needed, rate the strength of this source by circling a number between 1 and 5. Make notes on the thinking that supports your rating in the chart below.

Few Resources		Adequate Resources		Resource Rich
1	2	3	4	5

Type of Support Needed	Budget Range	Potential Source

Worksheet 4-3

Asset Source 3: Process Skills

How strong is your community's knowledge about interest-based or dialogue processes for resolving conflicts? What types of processes have been used in your community in the past? Do you have skills in the areas of planning, implementing, monitoring, and evaluating public engagement processes? What percentage of your population has the listening, critical thinking, and articulation skills needed for effective participation or the willingness to learn them? What resources are available in or to your community to provide information, facilitation, training or planning? After assessing the types of skills needed and where they might be accessed, rate the strength of this source by circling a number between 1 and 5. Make notes on the thinking that supports your rating in the chart below.

Limited Knowledge		Adequate Knowledge		Strong Knowledge
1	2	3	4	5

Skill Needed	Who Has	How Provide

Worksheet 4-4

Asset Source 4: Networks and Relationships

What types of relationships exist among different groups in the community, and how are those groups networked? Are there one or two groups that tend to dominate conversations on issues like economic development, public health, or safety, or do many contribute? How do groups interact? Do they compete, collaborate, or each work in a silo? In addition to civic groups like Chambers of Commerce, Rotary, Kiwanis, etc. do you have active and cooperative neighborhood associations or other grassroots community groups? How do the various groups interact with the government leaders in the community, how often, and on what issues? How effective are they in making their concerns heard or in implementing solutions? After assessing the types of groups that are active in your community and their interaction, both with each other, and with their government, rate the strength of this source by circling a number between 1 and 5. Make notes on the thinking that supports your rating in the chart below.

Limited Relationships		Some Groups Have Strong Interaction and Relationships		Strong Networks Involving Many Groups
1	2	3	4	5

Key Groups	Interact With	Compete or Opposed To

Worksheet 4-5

Asset Source 5: Vision

How strong is your community's shared vision for the future? Do leaders argue over competing visions? Do residents have a common direction and goals? Do residents have similar hopes or fears? Have some groups clearly articulated a vision that has garnered some community support? Has the community been through a process that resulted in a clearly articulated shared vision? Has the community ever discussed its vision? After assessing what, if any, visions have been publicly discussed and the depth of their support, evaluate this source by circling a number between 1 and 5. Make notes on the thinking that supports your rating in the chart below.

No Common Vision		Some Community Groups Share Vision		Clearly Articulated, Shared Vision
1	2	3	4	5

Future Vision	Who Has Articulated	Who Supports

Worksheet 4-6

Asset Source 6: Sense of Community

To what extent do members of your community have shared interests and values, a strong sense of place, or shared history? What historic experiences have divided the community or established bonds? Has your population been steady or experienced rapid growth with many newcomers? Would the majority of citizens define what it means to be a community in the same way? Are there any significant minorities with an incompatible view? Is the population as a whole inclusive and cohesive, or dispersed and competitive? What kind of language is used to describe other groups within the community – for example, do you hear more "we" or "us v. them"? After assessing these factors, rate the strength of this source by circling a number between 1 and 5. Make notes on the thinking that supports your rating in the chart below.

No Sense of Community		Some Shared Values and History		Clearly Articulated, Widely Shared Sense of Community
1	2	3	4	5

Shared Interests, Values, History Etc.	Language Cues	Divisions or Competition

Worksheet 4-7

Asset Source 7: Past Experience

What past experiences has the community had in resolving difficult issues together? Did past efforts at "public engagement" result in actual changes in policies or services aligned with public input or was public engagement viewed as "window dressing" used to support a preordained result? Did efforts to engage result in political retaliation or scapegoating of one or more groups? How inclusive were past processes? Were new relationships formed or existing hierarchies reinforced? Are the same people seen over and over in public input or do the number and variety of people involved continue to increase? Or has there been a decrease in participation? After assessing the efficacy, inclusiveness, openness, and transparency of past efforts at public engagement, rate the level of trust citizens are likely to have in public engagement processes by circling a number between 1 and 5. Make notes on the thinking that supports your rating in the chart below.

Past Failures		Mixed Experience		Past Success
1	2	3	4	5

Past Conflict	How Resolved	Factor in Current Conflicts

Worksheet 4-10

Asset Source 10: Civic Participation

How interested and willing are your citizens in working to improve civic life within your community? What percentage of citizens in your community regularly vote? How many volunteer with service projects or organizations? How many participate in civic engagement processes designed to help with policy development? Do citizens provide feedback on the implementation of policies or services? In what ways? To what extent are citizens either aware of their rights, or feel empowered to contribute? How well do citizens understand the systems of government, and how effective are they at accessing them? Do citizens believe their efforts can make a difference in how decisions are made or do they frequently express cynicism about the efficacy of involvement? After assessing the nature, frequency, and quality of citizen involvement within your community, rate the strength of this source by circling a number between 1 and 5. Make notes on the thinking that supports your rating in the chart below.

Very Minimal If Any Involvement In Civic Groups, Voting, Or Other Processes		Many Active Service Groups; A Stable Percentage of Citizens Regularly Vote, And Otherwise Engage		More Than 50% of The Adult Population Is Active In Service Groups, Voting, and Seeks Out Opportunities To Engage
1	2	3	4	5

Type Of Participation	Groups Participating	Participation Rate

Worksheet 4-11 – Summary and Calculation

Now that you have assessed the overall assets available to your community, you need to determine your overall asset score.

Asset Source 1: Information = ___

Asset Source 2: Monetary and In-Kind Resources = ___

Asset Source 3: Process Skills = ___

Asset Source 4: Networks and Relationships = ___

Asset Source 5: Sense of Community = ___

Asset Source 6: Shared Vision = ___

Asset Source 7: Past Experience = ___

Asset Source 8: Leadership = ___

Asset Source 9: Systems = ___

Asset Source 10: Civic Participation ___

Subtotal: ___

Divide by 10 for
Average of Asset Sources = ___

Now divide this average by 5 and multiply by 100 in order to put the Asset Score on a comparable percentage basis to the Conflict Score so they can be summed.

(Asset Average____/5) * 100 = _______ **ASSET SCORE**

Your Asset Score should be written into the equation on page 5 to finish calculating your Civic Health Diagnostic Score.

General Notes - Assets:

Our greatest assets are:

We can use these assets in the following ways:

We can maintain and further improve these assets by:

General Notes - Continued:

Areas in which we need to strengthen our assets are:

We can strengthen these assets by:

Strengthening these assets will help us to:

Part 5: Conflict Score Worksheets

This set of worksheets will provide the information needed to calculate your Conflict Score. The Conflict Score is a function of both the number and intensity of conflicts affecting the community. As stated previously, "conflict" is defined for purposes of this workbook as a significant difference among two or more groups in the community. These are conflicts that not only causes friction between groups, they raise emotions within the broader community, and erode trust in the community's leadership if not effectively resolved.

Begin by first identifying the major areas of conflict in your community. Note that the term "area of conflict" is broader than the specific interrelated issues that fall within that area of conflict. For example, multiple issues relating to planning and zoning, or new infrastructure, could be grouped together under "Growth and Development". Other areas of conflict might include "Crime", or "Law Enforcement", or "Environment". These can be areas where there are current disputes between groups or areas where conflicts regularly recur, even though there may not be a current conflict. Or the area may represent an emerging source of conflict – one in which complaints are often heard and there is general unease around topics that leaders in the community avoid talking about.

Identify no more than 5 of these general areas. You will fill out worksheets 5-1 through 5-6 for each of the conflict areas identified. These worksheets will help you group and identify the source of specific conflicts within the area. The core sources of conflict within each area are differences in (i) information, (ii) interests, (iii) values, and (iv) view of the relationship, and (v) systemic or structural issues. The number of issues arising within each area under each source will be related to a 1 to 5 scale, and the scale values will be summed across all areas first by source and then in total on worksheet 5-7.

Areas of conflict in our community include:

1.

2.

3.

4.

5.

Rating Conflict Intensity

As you go through the worksheets, you will also rate the intensity of conflict for each set of issues within an area on a scale of 1 to 5.

The intensity scale runs from Calm to Very Hot. Calm reflects genuinely friendly relationships where mutual respect and confidence that problems can be reasonably resolved are present. Relationships that are strained although cordial, or disinterested and avoidant, would fall somewhere between Calm and Heated. Heated can be characterized by clear expressions of anger or fear, the use of accusatory or mildly inflammatory language, and groups beginning to separate into "us" and "them" camps. "Hot" is a stronger version of Heated, although less than Very Hot. Very Hot would include physical threats, characterization of those in other groups as enemies, name calling (especially among leaders) and use of highly inflammatory language.

Calm	Warm	Heated	Hot	Very Hot
1	2	3	4	5

These scale values will also be summed across all areas first by source and then in total on worksheet 5-8. The final values from worksheets 5-7 and 5-8 will be used in worksheet 5-9 to calculate the overall conflict score.

Work sheet 5-1 – Area of Conflict: ______________________________

(Identify General Conflict Area (i.e. Development, Governance, Law Enforcement, etc) for worksheet set here)

Key Issues. Identify the key issues that regularly arise in this area. As you think about these issues ask yourself: what topics or challenges arise repeatedly? In what context? How are these issues stated? Are they argued in highly partisan terms or are those involved able to analyze it together? What parties make these claims or encourage these arguments? The more detail that you can recall about these conflicts the better prepared you will be to work through the related worksheets. Complete worksheets 5-2 through 5-6 for this same area. Once you have completed worksheets 5-2 through 5-6 for each of the areas listed on page 23, use worksheets 5-7 through 5-9 to calculate your conflict score.

1. Issue:

Notes:

2.Issue:

Notes:

3.Issue:

Notes:

4.Issue:

Notes:

5.Issue:

Notes:

Worksheet 5-2 Area of Conflict :______________________________

Sources of Conflict: Information

What conflicts are there regarding "the facts" of the issue at hand? What information or data is available and being used? What assumptions or claims are being made but not supported? Where do the groups get their information and how do they use it? Indicate which groups are making what claims. Be as specific as possible as this information will help you better understand the overall conflict. Then also note the intensity of conflicts over information. You can find a description of the intensity scale on page 24. Also make notes on the observed behaviors that support your intensity rating.

Claim	Information Used	Groups Asserting

Number of Conflicts Over Information (circle one):

1 to 2	3 to 4	5 to 7	8 to 9	10 or more
1	**2**	**3**	**4**	**5**

Intensity of Conflicts Over Information (circle one):

Calm		Heated		Very Hot
1	**2**	**3**	**4**	**5**

Observed Behaviors:

Worksheet 5-3 Conflict Area: ______________________________

Sources of Conflict: Interests

What conflicts are there over different interests in this area? This can, for example, be a difference between one group that wants to keep land open and another that wants to build on the land, or a difference between groups on allocating available funds between the arts or social services. List the interests being asserted and the groups that assert them. Be as specific as possible as this information will help you better understand the overall conflict. Then also note the intensity of conflicts over interests. You can find a description of the intensity scale on page 24. Also make notes on the observed behaviors that support your intensity rating.

Interest	Groups Asserting

Number of Conflicts over Interests (circle one):

1 to 2	3 to 4	5 to 7	8 to 9	10 or more
1	**2**	**3**	**4**	**5**

Intensity of Conflicts Over Interests (circle one):

Calm		Heated		Very Hot
1	**2**	**3**	**4**	**5**

Observed Behaviors:

Worksheet 5-4 Conflict Area: ____________________

Sources of Conflict: Values

What conflicts revolve around the values held by the parties involved in the issue at hand? List the values or principles being asserted in support of various claims and the groups asserting them. Sometimes groups that have opposed interests will have similar underlying values, such as a value for maintaining "green space". Be as specific as possible as this information will help you better understand the overall conflict. Then also note the intensity of conflicts over values. You can find a description of the intensity scale on page 24. Also make notes on the observed behaviors that support your intensity rating.

Value/Principle	Groups Asserting

Number of Conflicts Over Values (circle one):

1	2 to 3	4 to 5	6 to 7	More than 7
1	**2**	**3**	**4**	**5**

Intensity of Conflicts Over Values (circle one):

Calm		Heated		Very Hot
1	**2**	**3**	**4**	**5**

Observed Behaviors:

Worksheet 5-5 Conflict Area: ____________________________

Sources of Conflict: Systems or Structures

What conflicts are there over the rules, laws, boundaries and process in this area? Are the rules clear or misunderstood? Is application even-handed? Are the 'rules' accepted or viewed as unfair, operating to the benefit of certain groups and to the detriment of others? List the arguments that are being made about structures, laws, rules, systemic unfairness, etc. and the groups asserting those arguments. Be as specific as possible as this information will help you better understand the overall conflict. Then also note the intensity of conflicts over these systems or structures. You can find a description of the intensity scale on page 24. Also make notes on the observed behaviors that support your intensity rating.

Systemic Issues	Groups Asserting

Number of Conflicts Over Systems or Structures (circle one):

1	2	3	4	5 or more
1	**2**	**3**	**4**	**5**

Intensity of Conflicts over Systems or Structures (circle one):

Calm		Heated		Very Hot
1	**2**	**3**	**4**	**5**

Observed Behaviors:

Worksheet 5-6 Conflict Area: ______________________________

Sources of Conflict: Relationships

What conflicts arise in the relationships between the different parties in the issue at hand? This can involve groups identifying others as "enemies" or "friends" or different views of how certain individuals or groups "should" interrelate. What relationships, both positive and negative, are there among those involved? Note both the groups that are in conflict and those that work well together. Be as specific as possible as this information will help you better understand the overall conflict and provide some sense of how to approach different groups as you move forward with public engagement. Then also note the intensity of conflicts in these relationships. You can find a description of the intensity scale on page 24. Also make notes on the observed behaviors that support your intensity rating.

Groups	In Conflict With	Working Relationship With

Number of Relationship Conflicts (circle one):

1 to 2	3 to 4	5 to 7	8 to 9	10 or more
1	2	3	4	5

Intensity of Relationship Conflicts (circle one):

Calm		Heated		Very Hot
1	2	3	4	5

Observed Behaviors:

Worksheet 5-7 – Sources of Conflict Number Scores

Now that you have assessed the conflicts that arise across a variety of community issues, it is time to look at the number of conflicts, both within each source area, and across the board. Fill in the "Number of Conflicts" scale values for each area and source.

Once you have filled in the numbers for each area, you will then take an average of the scale values within each source, across the areas reviewed. Five blanks are provided although you may have identified and assessed fewer areas than that. If you have a score for only one area, use that number as your average. If you assessed less than 5 areas, use the number of areas (2, 3 or 4) that you did assess when calculating your average within each source.

Sources of Conflict: Information
Area 1 = ___ Area 2 = ____ Area 3 = ____ Area 4 = ____ Area 5 = ____

Conflict Number Average for Information (I) = ____

Sources of Conflict: Interests
Area 1 = ___ Area 2 = ____ Area 3 = _____ Area 4 = ____ Area 5 = ____

Conflict Number Average for Interests (N) = ____

Sources of Conflict: Values
Area 1 = ___ Area 2 = ____ Area 3 = ____ Area 4 = ____ Area 5 = ____

Conflict Number Average for Values (V) = ____

Sources of Conflict: Systems or Structures
Area 1 = ___ Area 2 = _____ Area 3 = ____ Area 4 = ____ Area 5 = ____

Conflict Number Average for Systems (S) = _____

Sources of Conflict: Relationships
Area 1 = ___ Area 2 = _____ Area 3 = ____ Area 4 = ____ Area 5 = ____

Conflict Number Average for Relationships (R) = ____

Finally, take the average of these averages (add averages values listed above, and divide by 5). Then multiply this value by the total number of Conflict Areas reviewed (1, 2, 3, 4, or 5):

(I + N + V+ S+ R)/5 * (Number of Areas) = ____ Conflict Number Score

Transfer your conflict number score to Worksheet 5.9. Then calculate your intensity factor score using worksheet 5.8

Worksheet 5-8 – Intensity Factor

The method for calculating your overall intensity factor is similar to that used for the Conflict Number Score. Fill in below the "Intensity" scale values for each area and source marked on worksheets 5-2 through 5-6.

Once you have filled in the numbers for each area, take an average of the scale values within each source, across the areas reviewed. Five blanks are provided although you may have identified and assessed fewer areas than that. If you have a score for only one area, use that number as your average. If you assessed less than 5 areas, use the number of areas (2, 3 or 4) that you did assess when calculating your average within each source.

Sources of Conflict: Information Intensity Factors:

Area 1 = ____ Area 2 = ____ Area 3 = ____ Area 4 = ____ Area 5 = ____

Average Information Intensity Score (I) = ___

Sources of Conflict: Interests Intensity Factors:

Area 1 = ____ Area 2 = ____ Area 3 = ____ Area 4 = ____ Area 5 = ____

Average Interests Intensity Score (N) = ___

Sources of Conflict: Values Intensity Factors

Area 1 = ____ Area 2 = ____ Area 3 = ____ Area 4 = ____ Area 5 = ____

Average Values Intensity Score (V) = ____

Sources of Conflict: Systems or Structures Intensity Factors

Area 1 = ____ Area 2 = ____ Area 3 = ____ Area 4 = ____ Area 5 = ____

Average Systems Intensity Score (S) = ___

Sources of Conflict: Relationships Intensity Factors

Area 1 = ____ Area 2 = ____ Area 3 = ____ Area 4 = ____ Area 5 = _____

Average Relationships Intensity Score (R) = ____

Finally, take the average of these averages and you have your intensity factor.

(I+ N+ V+ S+ R)/5 = _____ Intensity Factor

This sum should be transferred to Worksheet 5.9.

Worksheet 5-9 - Conflict Score Calculation

Use this worksheet to calculate the Conflict Score used in the equation on page 5. The Conflict Score is a function of both the frequency and intensity of conflict. The basic equation can be stated as follows:

$$\frac{\text{Frequency of Conflict} \times \text{Intensity of Conflict}}{125} \times 100 = \text{Conflict Score}$$

In this equation the Conflict Number Score from worksheet 5.8 and the Intensity Factor from worksheet 5.9 are multiplied, then divided by 125, which is the total possible number of points available, and multiplied by 100 to create a percentage that can be deducted from the Asset Score percentage:

(Conflict Number Score from 5-7 ____ x Intensity Factor from 5-8 ____)/125 * 100 =

______ Conflict Score

Insert this Conflict Score in the equation on p. 5 in order to finish calculating your Civic Health Diagnostic Score.

Area of Conflict Notes:

Our most intense conflicts are in the following areas:

Our most frequent conflicts are in the following areas:

Interrelationships between conflict areas include:

Intensity of Conflict Notes:

Our most frequent conflicts involve the following sources: (Note – If a source of conflict is common among all areas, that indicates an issue for which there might be a systemic fix. If present in less than all, consider why conflicts arise from this particular source in some areas and not in others.)

Our most intense conflicts involve the following sources: (Note – Analyzing if and how the intensity of conflict varies by conflict source, both within and among areas, can help to identify the potential for "flare-ups" when planning dialogues.)

What assets can help us to manage the intensity of our conflicts?

Part 6: Sample Calculations and On-line Resources

We have posted sample worksheet calculations for two different hypothetical communities using the worksheet format set forth in this workbook. The worksheet text that provides direction and guidance for filling out the worksheets is not reproduced in the examples.

We have also posted a list of on-line resources that you may find helpful as you plan for public engagement. This list includes three types of resources, (I) sites that generally compile resources, (ii) sites that provide detailed examples of public engagement processes and plans, and (iii) some on-line tools that can assist your planning.

You can also view resource updates and download some planning checklists and view other resources on the resource page of our blog:

www.buildingdialogue.wordpress.com/resources

Part 7: Afterword And Acknowledgments

Civic health, like physical health, can't be taken for granted. Good health, both civic and physical, improves quality of life. Our mobile, diverse, competitive, entertainment-oriented, distractable, and optimistic culture presents many challenges for maintaining civic life. Yet these same factors, when well-engaged, also provide the seeds for great achievements:

> "Democracy does not give the people the most skillful government, but it produces what the ablest governments are frequently unable to create, namely an all-pervading and restless activity, a super abundant force, and an energy which is inseparable from it and which may, however unfavorable circumstances may be, produce wonders. These are the true advantages of democracy."
>
> *Alexis de Toqueville, Democracy in America, 1835*

To achieve our country's ideal of "one nation, indivisible, with liberty and justice for all", we need leaders with both the desire and the skills to equip, engage, and empower the public. These skills include patience, perseverance, attention to detail, analytic and integrative thinking skills, and the ability to listen to and work with those with whom we may disagree. Productive dialogue both teaches and engages all of these factors, and more, for the benefit of the entire community.

> "We will only attain freedom if we learn to appreciate what is different, and muster the courage to discover what is fundamentally the same. America's diversity offers so much richness and opportunity. Take a chance won't you? Knock down the fences which divide."
>
> *Justice Thurgood Marshall*

We wish you well as you work to improve or maintain your community's civic health.

In addition to those resources cited elsewhere in this workbook, we would like to acknowledge the following authors for works that contributed to our thinking:

- The Aspen Institute's Rural Economic Policy Program for their 2001 report titled "Measuring Community Capacity Building."

- Christopher W. Moore for his 1996 book The Mediation Process: Practical Strategies for Resolving Conflict.

- Daniel Yankelovich for his 1999 book The Magic of Dialogue and his publication of the "Learning Curve."

- Dante Chinni and James Gimpel for their 2010 book Our Patchwork Nation: The Surprising Truth About the "Real" America.

- Eric Lotke and Robert Gerson from the Campaign for America's Future and Paul Waldman and Andrew Seifter from Media Matters for America, for the 2007 report titled "The Progressive Majority: Why a Conservative America is a Myth."

- Nathan Kirkpatrick for his September 14, 2010 article in *Faith and Leadership* titled "The leader and the loyal opposition."

- The National Ministries Division of the Presbyterian Church (U.S.A.) for its Conflict Intensity Chart.

- The GSA Office of Citizen Services and Communications for its 2009 report titled "Increasing Citizen Engagement in Government."

- Harris Interactive for "Civics Education", a report prepared for the American Bar Association, July 2005.

- The International Association of Public Participation for its 2007 "Spectrum of Public Participation."

- Ken Cloke for his 2001 book Mediating Dangerously.

- Richard Harwood and the Kettering Foundation for the 2005 book Hope Unraveled: The People's Retreat and Our Way Back.

- Stephen Covey for his 2006 book The Speed of Trust.

- The Herrmann Institute's "Whole Brain Thinking®" framework, www.hbdi.com

We would also like to thank our friends and families, especially Sarah's husband David Read, who encouraged us in the writing of this workbook and our related work.

-End-

About the Authors

Sarah J. Read, president of The Communications Center, Inc., has more than 25 years experience in helping others resolve complex issues. Sarah's clients have included both large and small businesses, professional firms, non-profits, community groups, educational institutions and governmental organizations. The matters she has worked on include large complex regulatory and legislative disputes, visioning and strategic planning efforts, and community dialogues. She has also helped many boards and teams improve the way they work together and their ability to collaborate with others. Sarah served on the Missouri Supreme Court Commission on Alternative Dispute Resolution, and has been an invited speaker on collaborative governance , civic engagement, and conflict resolution at several conferences, including conferences hosted by the Missouri Municipal League and the Central Indiana Chapter of the Association of Government Accountants. She has received numerous professional awards and recognitions, including an AV® Preeminent™ rating by Martindale Hubbell, recognition by her peers as one of the Best Lawyers® in Administrative/Regulatory Law, and by Corporate Counsel magazine as a "Top Lawyer" in Energy, Environmental and Natural Resources Law.

Dave Overfelt is an Associate Consultant with The Communications Center, Inc. and a Visiting Assistant Professor of Sociology at the Rochester Institute of Technology, working with the Urban and Community Studies program. Dave works with dialogue based urban development processes and his research emphasizes the need for the sciences to engage with their broader communities. He has published many articles, most recently "Planning for Possibility: Opening Democracy in an Ordinary City" in *Critical Sociology* . He was, along with David Brunsma and Steven Picou, an editor for *The Sociology of Katrina: Perspectives on A Modern Catastrophe, Vol. 1 and 2*, published by Rowman & Littlefield in 2010. He received his B.A. in sociology, Magna Cum Laude with honors, his M.A. in sociology, with honors, and his Ph.D., with honors, from the University of Missouri. In addition to teaching and researching, Dave has spent the last several years working as a facilitator for community dialogues, strategic planning processes, diversity programs, and other complex engagement processes involving small and large groups.

www.ingramcontent.com/pod-product-compliance
Lightning Source LLC
LaVergne TN
LVHW080527210926
848481LV00022B/3643